Playground of the Mind

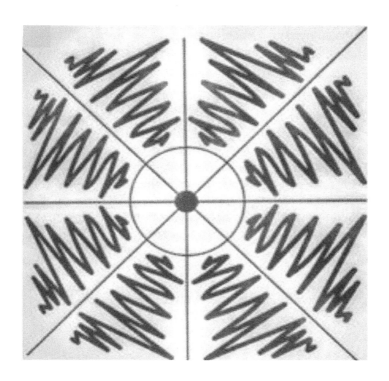

a View from a Servant/Warrior

Rafael Acosta Melendez

Book 1 of 3 ~ a Playground for Growth Series

This is an educational
and pleasure work of real life.
The events and characters described herein are
not intended to refer to specific places or living persons.
The opinions expressed in this manuscript are solely the opinions
of the author and do not represent the opinions or thoughts of
the publisher. The author has represented and warranted full
ownership and/or legal right to publish all the
materials in this book.

Nova Publishing & Book Store, Bakersfield, California
http://www.novapublishing.org
Nova Publishing and the "*NOVA*" logo are service marks
belonging to Nova Publishing.org
Bakersfield, California

Dedication

My Grandparents Leonidas Acosta and Josefina Esparza. These two took a chance in search for a better life for their family, traveled into the United States of America. They followed the process set forth in their minds. So that their family would have an opportunity to experience the American way of a life. Not knowing the language, not knowing what to expect and without transportation, they still persevered.

To my parents, Alberto Nila Melendez and Refugia de Maria Acosta for giving me life. These two migrated to wherever the work took them. From Texas to California for sure, and maybe many other states within the USA.

Their decisions and this book give thanks to My Family and My Friends. To the people where our paths crossed.

Without all of you. The playground in my mind would have been incomplete.

MY WIFE

Special thanks to Lorraine. A beautiful person since the day we met. And that has been over 40 years.

She understood and allowed me latitude from our family to venture out and get involved. With her understanding and encouragement, my playground stretches from Federal, State, and local government involvement. As well as from the streets to the waters around the world.

I married Lorraine when I was a student in high school, only 17 years of age.

Today, I am very thankful for the decision I made at so young of age.

That Credit goes to mom and dad.
Those two instilled the importance of hard work and praise to God.
Even today I find myself finally understanding what dad had said many years ago.

"Learn how to work."

Today, as I reflect I come to realize, at 17 years of age, I made decisions that shape my life throughout the course of my journey.

I took responsibility at a very young age and made decisions based on very few choices.

1. Married.
2. Enlisted in the United States Army.
3. Had an afternoon job.

   All while a senior in high school.

Since then, decisions I made had to be calculated to the best of my ability.
True, many were on the negative side, meaning those benefits were not going to work for our best interest. So, I stood a while, took the experience and moved on.
But many decisions that were made were definitely on the positive side.

   And to date are still rewarding.
Because of Lorraine's help, support and understanding, I was able to live my life to the fullest, while she created a home for us.

FAMILY

My family has always been there for me when I needed them the most. Family is family. And they are the ones you can count on at any time.

Here is where you will learn caring, love, and respect and how God plays a role in your life. Including the importance of hard work, where we came together to overcome the odds.

I hope, I have expressed my love toward them adequately and hope I have said I love them enough.

But I sure hope they felt my love and also know that I will always be there for them. And will always want the best for them.

My love also goes to my added family which includes my in-laws. Without them, Lorraine wouldn't have been around.
Cherish the moments with your family.

Once the family tree is cut down, it may not grow back.

This starts from the very beginning when Grandpa and Grandma made a decision to migrate into the United States of America with their family From Aguascalientes, Mexico. And Dad who also made a decision at a very young age to come North from Leon Guanajuato, Mexico.

With minimal skills and limited expectations their travels paid off.

<u>FRIENDS</u>

Some friends just become like family, caring and watching out for your best interest. Assisting and helping wherever they can, I cherish those friends.

They truly helped make my journey pleasant and enjoyable. My friends are the best you will ever find.

 I thank them for the time that was shared. For the hangouts in every shape, form or fashion. For the project where we work together for the betterment of others. From the most difficult to the most pleasurable times. The bonds that have been build will always be appreciated. I have great respect for the talents they carry and the talents they are willing to share.

Each and every one of them, played a role in developing my character.

Friends are special. They are not just acquaintances or fly by nights. We broke bread together and invested some time in developing a friendship. We can't control time, but we do have a choice on how we handle it.

These types of friends care about what happens to you and are concerned for your well-being. They defend you when others choose to turn their backs. Understand you and will be ok with your personality and your way of life.

This thought process, I have definitely always respected!

"If friendship had a price tag, I wouldn't be able to afford them."

This is what friendship sounds like when written in words.

Our Family, Friends, Our home, Our lives are where I have developed and gained the insight to these notes I will share with you throughout this reading.

- ➢ Don't allow work to become your dictator.
- ➢ Take control and put your skills on display. People will notice.
- ➢ Others won't have a clue.
- ➢ Stay confident and on path toward your place where you choose to be, it will become obtainable.

"Playground of the Mind"

Table of Contents

Introduction

Chapters

INTRODUCTION

As I navigated through life, I accumulated many notes. I have been involved in many different experiences. As I reflect, I cherish all those memories, whether positive or negative for they all played a role in my lifetime.

Hello;

I hope you find these notes helpful and maybe they will save you some precious time and avoid some unwelcome situations.

From the moment that I made those decisions at a young age, I gained knowledge and began to understand responsibilities and accept consequences. I endured much pain and frustrations as well as enjoyments and rewards.

As a Mayor of a small community I chose to take on the fiduciary responsibility of the community. As Master Sergeant in the United States Army, now retired, this is where I trained and assured soldiers followed and understood their responsibilities to the constitution. They always trained to standard and not to time. As I worked in a business setting, I was expected to employ my skills in leading a team toward the company's goals. Where I trained and ensured policy and procedure were followed. To take caution of safety issues and keep them the employees motivated so the goals of the company would always be met.

As part of any team that needs to meet expectations of the plans and goals set forth, my military training played a major role.

At times I stood back and allowed others to take the lead. At a set time they too may want to lead a team to meet deadlines, stay within budget, and set a pleasurable working environment.

I have always said, "If you know where you are going, then by all means lead."

Lead, follow, or get out of the way.

Education is necessary in order to know and understand the different requirements in different fields. You will find there are rules and regulations one must adhere to. Policies and procedures in order to control set outcomes, as well as laws in order to avoid disruption. Also, protocol and ethics to understand and become accepted.

All the same to learn and grow by, but different. As you grow and decide to take on new responsibilities, you'll find that you may not be accepted till you have proven yourself.

Picture this! At the time when I received my first permanent duty station in the United States Army, I felt like a tourist in a foreign country. To everyone there, I was the 'new guy'. When the more seasoned soldiers walked past me, It was as though their eyes were piercing right through me.

Once I had spent time in a live mission training exercise they saw what I was capable of. Things began to change. I can still feel the effects of my commanding officer shouting in my face. Not just for the sake of those Vietnam Veterans hearing their own roar! But for my own safety there is NO room for error when it came to my fellow soldiers lives.

As time went on, I noticed I was given additional responsibilities as the Veterans watched at how self-assured I was learning to survive. Before long I found myself invited to share some down time within the team circle. That's how I knew I was in.

Hopefully you will sense how continuous education played a major role toward my playground. You may find these notes as a refresher course. Or use them to assist in development and accomplishments toward your next responsibility.

It's a handy compact book with appropriate, useful information.

Let's get your playground started.

Life in itself is bigger than we could imagine. Your mind has the capabilities to consume everything you are willing to feed it. The more tools and experience you are willing to deposit

into it, the bigger your playground will become!

We all have different routes to navigate, yet we all begin with the same basic concept. From standing on our own two feet, to receiving assistance as we try to balance when we first begin to learn to ride a bike. We are taught and receive assistance in accomplishing our goals. There has always been people in your life willing to help, if you are willing to ask. As you continue your reading, you will find A note to understand Maslow's Hierarchy of needs.

Where the required survival skills are prioritized. A purpose to sustain a livelihood and updating our educational skills. To stay informed and current and practice seeking opportunities to maintain our status quo.
Like everything in this life, nothing is probably the only thing that is free. Otherwise, you will need to sacrifice something or lose time doing it. Since we will expend the same amount of time doing nothing, why don't we put our skills to task and gain something?

Work is and *always will be work*. Until you discover the passion that will take you to different heights. That's when you will see the opportunities that will arrive as you travel through your path of employment. Then and only then will you be able to approach your work in a different mindset, at which time the enjoyment and the satisfaction will take a different meaning. The word "work" will take on entirely a different scope.

Life is your audience, whatever you say and/or do will have an effect on someone or something. How and what you wish to accomplish as you spend valuable time at work will depend on you. We all feed off different needs and different styles of motivation.

What will yours be? You'll have opportunities to try your skills here on your co-workers. Do you carry anything special or different? If you choose, you can share your talents to make your working environment smoother and pleasurable. Build a family environment. Whatever stage you wish to set; relax and enjoy the show.

The good thing you will receive is a 'free pass' every day if you show up. Also included is coffee, doughnuts and water if it's your choice. At times, you might even get a lesson to boot, on updated safety issue, or new equipment that will be required.

The enjoyment of all this at this point, you will find the "Playground of your mind" expanding. Enjoy the ride, and continue to take advantage of opportunities given to you. Those will contribute in building your playground.

CHAPTER ONE

SUCCESS, BALANCE, TRUST

SUCCESS: to happen or terminate according to desire. Whichever desire your goal may be, you will need to work toward it. Prepare yourself. Put some time into it and you will need to sacrifice. The sooner you find your passion the less sacrifices you might have to take.

Change your <u>A</u>ttitude. Build a <u>C</u>haracter. <u>E</u>njoy life. Become an ACE in your own thinking. The one thing in common in a working environment is:
- ➤ Everybody is qualified to do their job,
- ➤ Take care of their responsibility,
- ➤ Some better than others.

Take care of your responsibility and assure your duties are completed first and foremost. As you talk with others or volunteer for additional duties, assure you understand what you are getting into and who you are talking to. Always keep a positive mind set. Stay confident. After all, you are doing what you enjoy and there's no need to change that setting. If you choose to not take a chance or change your position, then leave well enough alone. Stay within your rim of expertise. Once you uncover the gifts of your passion. you will never work a day in your life.

At times when you expect more than you have control over, disappointment may set in. Don't let it overtake you. Back up and regroup and renew yourself.

There were many times where I felt disappointment. I figured every one of us was on the same sheet of music. These folks were educated, well versed. But for some unknown reason we couldn't meet half ways. Either I didn't make myself clear, or because I didn't understand my role, or they just couldn't relate. So I backed up and reassessed the situation and found another approach to relay my message. There are many different styles to accomplish any situation. You need to figure which one works best for you.

Enjoy your disappointment for a moment. You might learn something.

As I spoke about my disappointment above I found that even when you give credence to all involved, sometimes a closed mind doesn't allow for the best outcome of any situations. During the times of disappointments I had to rely on my training, my skills. I had to quickly assess the situation and maneuver in a different direction. I learn by moving quick, fast and in a hurry those skills I gather do precisely work. Without bad times. You will never see the beauty of the good times and the skills you harness.

Re-evaluate and move forward. Check if emotions are out of our control. Use caution when in an emotional state of mind. Try to avoid making decisions during this period. If and when you decide to react during this frame of mind and it's a negative response, you'll have to apologize and hope for the best. Brush yourself off and move on.

Time is one asset we do not have much of. Let's try to make the right choice in the first opportunity. Avoid having to do it again at double the cost of time.

Look around!

We all have difficulties; we all have struggles. Some may be smaller than others. Many people are always willing to help. They only have to be asked. Take the time to ask. Worst case scenario, they can only say no. Nothing lost. It's an answer. Learn from it. It's possible the person you asked didn't have an answer. You had given him or her too much credit. But now you have come to realize those folks can be all show and no sustained sustenance. A question never asked will never need to be answered.

If you aren't ready for the answer, don't ask the question. Simple!

Our movements will begin to cut multiple facets in our lives. And we will begin to recognize everybody has a direction they are heading toward.

Finding yours is the ultimate key

We all need each other. For example; The person who owns a restaurant does not get rewarded if there are not any patrons for him to serve. Another example; The entertainer doesn't make any wages, if there is no one to pay the price. Etc.; Without you, someone, or something, may not succeed. That's all I am saying.

Let's find balance;
One lesson that was very helpful in my travels was Maslow's Hierarchy of needs.

Google it . . .

Very insightful information. There are 5 levels of needs in his hierarchy.

First is <u>Physiological needs</u>, where you will find your need to survive. Like food, water, housing, and a place to rest. Once you have satisfied these needs at this level, and you have control of where they will come from. Only then will you be comfortable moving on to the next level. Even though you may find yourself stepping into the next levels during your trials. you will not be totally committed until the physiological needs are met.

Build with confidence.

Each goal in fulfilling your plan will take a different worth and the balance within you will be a challenge.

BALANCE

: a condition in which opposing forces are equal to one another.

A friend once said, *"You have to pick your poison."* If you can handle the worst minute, the worst day of anything, then maybe this is the excursion you might want to consider.

While in the military I once drove the company commander around on his personally assigned vehicle, an M151 jeep. As a unit we were expected to rotate this duty. Well I thought, hey good duty, ride around everywhere during training exercises. Instead of humping that 80-pound rucksack that I couldn't even lift while standing. I had to lay on my back, strap it on, then turn onto all fours (hands and feet) and raise myself in this manner.

Any ways, why not right? The only problem was, I slept a heck of a lot less and at one time while driving, I found myself braindead. That's when your eyes are open but can't see where you are going. This happen to me once.

One evening while driving the First Sergeant back to garrison to pick up the meals for the next morning, I mentioned to him that I couldn't see. He immediately took action. Calmly he instructed me to slow the vehicle down, and stop it. Then he reached over and turned it off. He came around the jeep and assisted me in unbuckling my seat belt . He then walked me around the jeep on to the passenger side and sat me down onto the seat, buckled me up and took over the duties of driver.

Immediately I was out, asleep. Thank god someone was with me who understood my predicament. Top shelve Vietnam Veteran. I learned my limits that day.

When I was humping those 80-pound rucks at least I was able to sneak in a nap. As the driver my required duties were to be at the ready, at all times to travel at any given moment of the day or night. Whenever the commander was called upon to attend a conference, and he had plenty. When I wasn't doing for him, I was traveling during the dark hours to pick up chow. With minimal sleep and always moving somewhere.

Yes I didn't have to hump that ruck, but after having spent some time as the company commanders driver, I learned very quickly that humping with an 80 pound rucksack was a heck of a lot better than driving around a commander. I guess I became accustomed to the work. Humping across swamps and at times enjoying a helicopter ride on those UH-1, Huey. Strapped in and with the side door open, allowed the wind to blow in your face. While appreciating the beautiful view of the horizon and enjoying the flying formation from both front and back, lowering and rising depending on the wood line. A lot of discipline was required, but sneaking in a nap was a little more rewarding. The poison was the humping but the reward and state of mind was camping.

Our motivational saying was "every day is a picnic, every weekend is a holiday", nothing changes, still had to hump that 80-pound rucksack; but with an adjusted attitude and a different state of mind.

Life was more accepting. I took advantage of the given situation (Commander's driver) and learned from it. I found I didn't enjoy it much so I moved out. And returned to a place I consider more appealing. Where I understood my role.

Decide on your next step. Evaluate which one will benefit you the most. Figure out how much time you are willing to allocate toward that move. The plan will take care of itself.

TRUST

*: Reliance on integrity, strength, ability, surety, of a person or thing; confidence.
Believe in yourself for we all have to travel trials and tribulations.*

Trust is a necessity to any decision you make. By adequate preparation and organization, sacrifice and discipline. You will find that many things are possible and many people are trustworthy. We are all in this together. We all need each other in some shape or form. Working together is necessary in order to achieve the common goal. Most of society is here to help in some shape, form or fashion. Be a part. Trust in yourself and the people with who you surround yourself. At the end of the day, that's all you really have.

Those that speak ill to you about others, Will speak ill to others about you.

CHAPTER TWO

Meeting of Writer's Mind

As I touch on some notes, you can start to assemble your own personal files. You see at 17 years of age; major decisions were made during my senior year of high school. My choices were few and I was young and green. Toward the end of the senior year, I was working a part time job four hours in the afternoon. I was already married and trying to finish high school, with my wife expecting a child.

That was my beginning.

I made the best decisions from the choices I had. I thought I had an idea of what was to come but as usual, I was kidding myself. I stood balanced right here because I had what I needed at this given time. I had enough on my plate. And yes, I had plenty of help from family and friends. Otherwise, it would have been difficult.

Everything I share with you are the notes on how society played a part in my growth. Married at 17, Retired by 53. No matter the circumstances, anything is possible. Access your thoughts and consume your surroundings.

By asking questions and expanding your boundaries you may find different interest and develop more choices. Walk softly, and speak with integrity. The only reaction you will receive is either positive or negative. How you handle them will be your choice. Adjust as necessary, and keep moving forward. Doesn't matter how fast or slow.

By moving forward, it will eventually get you there.

Upon graduation I looked forward to heading onto boot camp. I had registered to join the military at the beginning of my senior year. And now, the time had come to pay the price. On top of all that, our son was scheduled to be born on the 4th of July of that year. I asked if I could delay my departure date to wait for his arrival.

Thanks be to God, Yes! My wish was granted. Now, this meant everything would have to change. Otherwise. I would have to wait 3 months till the next scheduled class for Truck Driving Training. I didn't want to wait. I had responsibilities to account for. So, I asked another question. What courses are available? The answer was Infantry school! Be careful what you ask for. You just might get it!

I took this date and that's how I finally entered the United States Army.

INFANTRY, STRAIGHT LEG. (grunt)

Being trained by those hard-core Vietnam Veterans was an extreme education and an experience I won't likely forget. Or better yet, haven't forgotten. You could never satisfy those guys. When you thought you were good enough well, guess what. You are wrong for just thinking! The lesson learned was, 'always walk with your guard up'. Leave yourself an out. And always know the route. Be Prepared!

You are never done learning.
Until you live in an infantry unit where all they do is train for war, It's hard to describe. If I have to explain, you probably wouldn't understand. The brotherhood that develops is unexplainable. You wouldn't exchange it if given a choice. The Veterans in the military are good people who laugh from the heart.

Work hard and play harder.

I enjoyed a total of 28 years both reserve and active duty combined. I retired with the rank of Master Sergeant. I learned many limitations. But I also learned that I was capable of many things in many conditions. I Had strengths and knew my ability. Today from where I reflect upon this, I truly believe God had his hand on this. I truly had no clue what was expected of me. But as long as I followed orders and showed respect, I grew.

I remember one summer night while still in school. Finishing my junior year, I met Lorraine. I was one of the boys who helped her and her friends with their performing outfits and equipment. They were due to perform folkloric dancing at our local church. Lorraine enjoy dancing very much. I think that was what caught my eye. Now that I am looking back, my destiny was laid out.

As a senior in high school, I was married and had a job. I was also scheduled to head to the military after graduation. My entire world had taken a major shift. I thought I was ready. After I received the blessing from my parents. The one prayer I asked of God, just keep me working and everything will take care of itself. I didn't realize what I asked for that day. But I wouldn't change it for anything.

At the age of 53 I retired from my employment, as well as being retired from the military. I also performed the duties of the Mayor in a small community. And also served as a School Board Member, and currently serve as a councilmember. I mentor at the local school district, as well as assist in the CA Cadet school program. I continue to assist in some fashion, shape or form in bettering people's lives.

One thing for sure, be careful what you ask for. You just might get it. Ha-ha-ha.

I've had many excursions. Some I invested more time than in others. For instances, my employment, I spent over one-third of my time devoted to the company's cause. I am grateful for the opportunities which were given. The company showed me plenty of opportunities. Every one of those co-workers contributed something in preparation toward my retirement. Over 30 years employed at one company with personal growth is quite an accomplishment.

Next was the United States Army with 3 years of active duty and 25 years reserved. Again grateful. Third was where I volunteered as an elected public servant in my community for over 30 years. These are blessings.

Alongside of all this was my recreation, being a Gym Rat with a buddy at his homemade gym in a two-car garage. The dude was equipped. On my 50th Birthday I did join the 300-pound club.

That's where you bench press 300 lbs., at least once.

Also cycling with the neighbors on the road bikes (Bicycle) as we hauled them around the state and including Mexico, Baja California. I enjoyed playing billiards with some top shooters of the area. One of them was the state amateur champion. As a team we also Qualified for the Amateur championship in Las Vegas. Funny stuff, even landed in some movies as an extra. Met some Big Actors. A different crew of good people. Movies like "The Devil has a Name" directed by Edward James Olmos and the Movie "McFarland USA" with Kevin Costner and Maria Bello. Directed by Niki Caro.

Also took the opportunity of deep sea fishing with all those cool guys. It's always nice to do things with people who are prepared, and know what to expect.

Even found enjoyment heading to the barber and playing poker. But the best entertainment was Motorcycle riding, HD 2003 Softail Heritage. And to date we continue enjoying the ride. We experienced the ride to Sturgis, South Dakota. 75th anniversary Sturgis Motorcycle Rally. I believe the turnout at that time was 800,000 people or so. It is always a nice pleasure to ride with good friends. Brothers as we call each other. We have also made runs to Mexico and Canada. The local rides are where I visit with all the local biker brothers and also enjoy short trips to Laughlin, Nevada.

And Lorraine is there with me. Enjoying the ride, living our lives.

Lorraine is the mother of Ralphie our son, and Mona our daughter. She is grandmother to three Grandchildren, Isaac, Cristopher, and Nathan. These three are the best of my challenges today. I thank God for allowing all of you to be part of my life.

I am thankful for many errors I made. And grateful for all the rewards that were taken in turn. The only persons who make errors are those willing to try something new.

We are all in this together. Let's be discerning and accept and comprehend how all this works. You'll see, life is worth living. Good, Bad, or indifferent; live it to the best of your ability. With what you have control of.

Throughout life all of us will develop a character. You will meet so many distinct personalities through so many different venues. The only requirement of you will be to be willing to meet. And if necessary, ask questions.

Those resources will be valuable to you because of their experiences and knowledge, and for their assistance and guidance. New friends, new ideas, new sources, allow them to become part of your journey.

Looking back when we were young we played a lot of games. Which included running and yelling. Which were physical and challenging. All those games had rules and logic. All were a form of a test in developing growth. So Relax, it's nothing new. We have been learning since the beginning of our time.

Learning, growing, adjusting and seeking for 'a somewhere', finding your own way. It is incumbent for us to share our skills and assist in finding the next generation's balance. Since we are all different. I am hoping you begin to sense your importance as you navigate through the hardships as well as enjoy the rewards. Do it your way,

BECAUSE ALL THE OTHER LIVES ARE TAKEN.
And this one is yours.

Nothing is guaranteed. You do nothing, you gain nothing. Remember, this game is played till the end.

You see, the time I chose to sacrifice allowed me to enjoy many things. I took advantage of the opportunities given to me. And I appreciated all of them, including all the good people I met

along the way. These folks had their own style. Carried different attitudes. And their skills were unique to them. Because of their acceptance, I was able to enhance my playground. And began to realize and understand we are all seeking something and going somewhere in search of balance to enjoy our time sensibly. With these "uniqueness of thoughts", my playground of my mind broadened and became an area of information to draw from.

Today hard labor has subsided to a point. But without a strong work ethic, we will not survive. In order to gain something, you will need to lose something. As in life, If you are not working and instead choose to take advantage of a helpful hand and receive handouts, that's ok, but don't get stuck there. The hand that feeds you, can also starve you!

NOW WHAT.

Take the opportunities to grow and cultivate your abilities. For at some point, you will need the fruit they bare.

SACRIFICE
: to surrender or give up, or permit.

While seeking your next goal and carrying the load that you have access to. Finding a balance will become an absolute. Once your balance becomes defined, you will enter many different gateways. Always be prepared for what comes next. The patience you have displayed, will now be rewarded only if your time management skills are up to par. This will happen in accordance with your sacrifice and the choices you have gathered.

Life is an everlasting change. To think, one can possibly know everything there is to know, It's just not possible. The only thing constant in life is change. There are so many areas of interest to travel. I am certain in your lifetime; it is not possible to discover all of them. With all these different bodies and minds heading in multiple directions, You alone will not be able to monitor all of them .

What I do know is you need to learn the art of asking questions so you may discover and understand how you revolve around your world at this moment. With a little effort on your part and the passion in your heart, you will eventually arrive at your destination. Be prepared to take on opportunities that come your way. Finding enjoyment in this ride, it's not for the weak.

Sounds nice? Yeah.

Just like you have expectations of yourself, the world around you has expectations of its own. That is called decree. In every activity you take part in, they play by some rules, understandings or agreements. Expectations have always been required to avoid safety hazards, which come with rules and regulations. All the while, more information is offered as you move along.

The choice will be yours.

Different rules are required in different conditions. Simple fact. In order to assist in avoiding downtime, rules and limits are put in place. Everything in life is measured by someone or something.

Logic is the key I'll choose to use throughout this reading.

WELCOME TO
"THE PLAYGROUND of the MIND"

Reading, Writing, Arithmetic, Listening and Speaking are some key elements to help development of a character. The basic skills in everything. Which is the essential part of growing and continuance to move forward. As you enjoy this reading, I have taken the privilege in keeping notes for you.

This book is conveniently handy for quick reference.

CHAPTER THREE

SELF

Your journey should be about you working on your plan and getting the necessary information to get you there. It's like a road map with all these avenues but you just don't know where to go. (We will call them opportunities). You will have to select which one at any given moment is best suited to choose.

In the decision-making process, keep in mind, the past and the future as the choices you take, will assist you in getting through the present time.

Now, here is where your responsibility takes place. Being cognizant of your surroundings will be an essential trait to develop. Don't get caught by people who will play on words. They might come across as being humble. But in essence, their own poor souls deceive them. Take caution; with great knowledge comes greater responsibility. As much as you know, others might know just as much, or not. By the traits and principles, you will harness, and the skill of asking questions, you will come to find folks as such who pretend to be as equal as you. They will use tactics as, "dropping names", meaning, trying to lead you to believe they know people. Or present themselves as being in the know. Therefore, upon realization of this fact. Play along and make a determination of what information these kinds of folks are after, or trying to hide. As words can be deceiving, actions are a little more difficult to conceal.

Other things to consider will be:
- ➢ Volunteering, giving from the kindness of your heart, without expectations of rewards and recognitions.
- ➢ Your rewards will come in due time.
- ➢ Relax and enjoy your ride which is the essence of life.
- ➢ Share of yourself, payback, and feel the balance automatically form.

We all had different beginnings. What we do from this point forward will help develop a process which will aid you for the effects to come. Think about you first. If you are not at a balancing point, how will you be able to assist or help others? A ladder has rungs. Each step upward is one step closer to getting there. A rope? Well, you can climb it, maybe tie things with it. Or you can just hold it. Don't be a rope holder and wait for someone to pull it so you may take a step. A step that will be out of your control.

Please appreciate. A rope holder only holds on for dear life waiting for someone or something to change things for them. Oh yeah, those types of folks speak a good game. But as the story goes, their actions speak louder than words alone. During your infant years , when you were first encouraged to stand, someone assisted you. Someone had to help you understand the importance, the beauty of standing on your own two feet. As you developed strength and grew each day it made you more aware. You became creative and started holding on to chairs, sofas, even the legs of an adult. You raised yourself with your two arms if necessary. Encouragement and a little assistance has always been a part of your life.

When you fell? You learned to get back up and try again. Not succeeding at first is not failure. It's a level of understanding that you hadn't achieved. With a little effort and some training while keeping an open mind, and practice the day came when your confidence level advanced and you stood up. You were ready to take on new ventures, make some decisions and develop choices. First thing in life was to allow yourself to be taught. Then practice and prepare for the opportunity. Without a system or a process, it will make your life a little more challenging.

As you have found, living life is no easy task. Life is not for the weak minded. Many situations that will confront you have answers. You may come to not agree with all of them and that's ok. But as you will find, doing some reflections at any given point just might help in assuring you are walking the path you have planned.

Thinking about what went wrong or right is the best part in developing the mind. And will serve in developing a creative way of thinking.

We all have different styles and different approaches. We walk to a different beat. We find different waters to float our boat. We react to people with certain beliefs. Learn to adjust and adapt as you advance in life. You only have one.

Learn, Live and enjoy it.

Just like in the road map. You can always find another road to turn off and reset yourself if that particular choice didn't or doesn't work out for you.

it's never a loss to take a calculated chance. Only a gain of knowledge. Take one, it might become a lifetime reward. Life is set up for your success. The price you are required to pay is time, effort, and sacrifice. Develop a vehicle that you maintenance frequently, assuring all the lights are working and the horn works for when danger approaches. Keep the required tools clean for those unexpected moments. Your time is valuable.

Avoid downtime.

Life is very similar.

By staying healthy and updating your required information in the field of expertise will assist in finding your balance and to live your own life.

The world's a stage. What role do you have passion for? Play it! Be a part.

Find something you enjoy doing. Learn to do it very well. Then find somebody that needs your services and get rewarded for it.

Wonderful, Right?

CHAPTER FOUR

PLANNING

Planning is defined as: The act of process of making a plan. Stay within the scope of your plan and figure out how you will get there. Know the type of preparation that will be required and how you will accomplish this task. By being creative with your information, you can and will find an answer on how the first steps will be taken.

Planning is one of the required lessons you will find handy on your journey. With a plan, you will not only have an idea or expectations on how you will get there, but you will also know when you get there. Every plan is slightly different for the mere fact that we grew up in a different environment with different circumstances.

But we all have to go through a process in order to obtain any given result. The beauty of a plan is to think of it as a road map. You can always prepare one and if the anticipation isn't what you expected, back up and consider another. I say this, because as soon as you have it all figured out, conditions change.

When considering advice from outside sources be careful who those might be. Many people speak aimlessly and truly don't know the road you may seek. To tell someone to move accordingly will just not be possible. We all have different lives. Therefore , by communicating and asking questions you will be able to determine if the advice received will assist you as an individual on your personal venture.

One thing to assure when seeking a mentor is, does the individual comprehend my thoughts and am I capable of following through? This is a reason why every individual should design his own plan. As a mentor what I give in return is, I help guide and facilitate, as well as motivate toward accomplishing the plan.

Mentors help, assist and make the road of their mentees smoother, with least difficulties as possible to save them time and frustration. We plan by using everything we do. The environment and your surroundings, including the people you meet. In sharing these notes. Everything we do requires planning. As you can see, I have written these notes for you.

All That will be required of you is placing some effort into practice of writing up a plan. This book is written to help and assist you in understanding some important values that you may find essential to further help you climb your ladder of life. Sometimes by reflecting on your plan, you can analyze where you have been. Where you are at currently, and where you are headed. Take frequent stops and smell the roses. You might find that even a beauty of a rose grows on so many thorns.

 I had an opportunity to speak with a lady. She was feeling sad and couldn't understand why her situation of marriage had turn so sour. As she describes to me how terrible her life has been and why did it happen to her, she just couldn't understand. I said to her, you're walking in the travels of the Rose. She turned toward me in a stare, with her eyes asking the question of what! I continue with my story. and explained; You see life is like a Rose. sometimes we all have to travel through some thorns (trials and tribulations) in order to begin to smell that pleasant fragrance and feel the freshness amidst the air. When you reach the level of acceptance the view of the rose appears. You welcome it and bring it up close. The beauty of contentment feeds the soul, and your joy returns in fullness.

As we talked and I found out more about her. She and I came to realize, she is now in a better place than before. True, she thought she had gained something early in life. Yes, the gain quickly became a loss. But at the end when it was all said and done, she was ending up at a better place spiritually, mentally, and physically. When I left her, she remained with a smile on her face and hopefully with thought of understanding in her achievement.

Make a plan, at least you will know when you get there.

And live life.

<u>Understanding</u> *will require trial and error. Most of your time will be allocated toward the objective of understanding.*

Brush off any obstruction or circumstance that may obstruct your path toward accomplishing your plan and move on. Or make it right and feel better, but please find closure. At the end of the day, make mental notes on how your day went by giving yourself an after-action review. This is another way to better serve yourself. Planning is essential since conditions will change often. You will need to adjust your position frequently.

C H A P T E R   FIVE

APPLY YOURSELF

Etiquette: conventional requirements as to social behavior; properties of conduct as established in any class or community or for any occasion.

Your character will play a major role into entering those established communities. By developing relationships, you will find accessibility rewarding. Due to the fact of your understanding, effort and investment of time will always be a valuable expense. Your gain will be determined by what you are willing to sacrifice. Invest in yourself and take calculated chances. Using this method will grant you more gain than loss.

Interesting. Huh? Nothing is lost, only gained.

We have been through a state of logic our entire life. The decisions you make, either take you to your next desired place or it just may take you to a place of reflection. A place of study. Whichever the result, time and preparation are essential parts in the

Playground of your mind.

All of these notes, I have placed into practice in one form or another. As a retired Master Sergeant in the United States Army, I reflect on a phase that sticks in my mind. And was used often while serving in an Infantry unit.

Learn it, know it, live it. Or people die.

You see, there (military life) we lived by a different set of rules. Different expectations and requirements. Our lives focused on the mission at hand, And to win! By using those concepts here and now. In your current state of mind. Where wars shouldn't exist. Life should be less complex. We all have a mission to accomplish. Let's move on it together.

Stay focused and always be aware of your surroundings. Be careful on the words that you will use because in turn, some people might get hurt. At that given moment, it might not matter much. But that person could possibly make your journey easier and much more rewarding. You may possibly acquire a friend. I never took anything outside my home personally. Sure, you will always be tested. But by staying prepared, your disappointments will be minimized.

Sometimes, agreement on both sides is not possible for one reason or another. That's just nature. Compromise and watch the pieces fall into place. Sometimes it's better to agree to disagree and keep it moving! Nothing is a loss, whenever you have gained. Those that have gained knowledge are those that are willing to take a chance.

PRACTICE, SELF EVALUATE, ADJUST
And always give thanks
for all your opportunities.
You will either see them as they develop or you
will see them as they pass you by....

CHAPTER SIX

24 HOURS

Here is where you will develop your character.
Where you will apply your studies. Take a
chance, practice and learn. The playground is
where the decision you make will now have
ramifications that you yet haven't experienced.
Or maybe you have and will improve your
position. We all have 24 hours. What will you do
with yours? This will be totally up to you.
You have developed choices toward your goals
in life. Play them and find out if those are
sustainable. You have collected some essential
needs. Like Reading, Writing, and Arithmetic. In
this current age, life with the skills of writing ,
reading and arithmetic are very crucial. Survival
skills of hunting and building are still very much
relevant. And understanding of Rules and
Regulations in order to obtain a residual to
sustain our way of living to its fullest. In a
service society we need to incorporate the use

of technology and the internet where choices are bountiful. Without these three components, life becomes a little more challenging, but not impossible. By knowing how to read, currently everything can be brought up by simply asking for help. This "google" internet character gives us limitless access to help.

Assuring a basic education will save much time. Whether you call it advanced or additional education. It is still basic toward your interest. Learning to write is another way of communicating. Being able to convey a message in writing avoids any confusion or misunderstanding. By developing the sense of logic, through the use of arithmetic, while it develops your thinking pattern, you and those others will always have a common ground, of communicating. By simply knowing that facts are facts. When you come to realize that everything seems to be the same, but different, this will be a good sign of growth.

You have reached a level of acceptance,

where logic and basic instinct have welcomed each other. There are many things we need to understand. But in our case, understanding everything, is just not possible. Just like a playground where all of the equipment is new to a toddler and understanding it all at once is not possible. It takes time and patience to learn how to use the swings and the slide and the merry-go-round......

Let's get a basic understanding of some words. Words that will be in our programs and plans till the end of time. Words like ethics and protocol, rules and regulations, policies and procedures and laws of order. Now that you have accepted the concept of limitations, with some effort, life will begin to unfold. This is the time when your character should be adjusted or formed.

   If you would like to be understood, find the time to understand.

Find the passion in everything you do. Whether you found it positive or a negative or from a small role or a big one. It's all a test. It could lead to something different or become a piece needed in finishing your plan. There will be many who will advise you on how to go about something. They'll tell you what to expect. But truthfully, how could they, if they never experienced the issue from your shoes? Or from where you stand. Information of any sort could be useful with a creative way of thinking. This will assist you to better prepare yourself. Therefore, all information can be good information.

You don't know what you know until you know what you know.

You have been taught to think on a given pattern since the very beginning. From the time you were born. Through the streets you have walked. Everything you saw and who you talked to, have been lessons. Your eyes have gathered information based on your basic principles and values. Which may have been taught at home. Your ears have become honed in on the words delivered, and sensitive to the harshness or the gentleness of the tones heard. By adding your current environment into the equation, it begins to add up. A decision-making process has formed and choices will take place. As it became clearer, you began to choose which information is valid and which will be placed in a mental file, as you venture into different fields.

Time invested and the willingness to sacrifice will tell where you stand. You will choose from which values, principles and even relationships you will be devoted to. We all have 24 hours. By what you can see, it all has logic. Formed by rules and regulations. Moved by a basic approach. Only time will tell where it will end.

If you want to be understood, you need to take time to understand. That comes with sacrificing something, which will be time and something of value to you.

It's like an exchange market, a recycling center. Take something back and you will receive something in return. If you bring or give nothing, then expect nothing in return.

Let's talk about
VALUES;
LOYALTY: give your best if you chose to commit.
DUTY: complete your requirements
RESPECT: your ability and those of others.
HONOR: do the right thing at all times.
INTEGRITY: do the expected when no one is watching.
PERSONAL COURAGE: take a chance when you feel prepared.

All these values carry a significance in my growth and in everything I have chosen to do. If I couldn't agree and or couldn't defend my values, then I would find the courage to remove myself from there, before I surrendered to any entity. I first did my homework. I researched beforehand to the best of my ability. Yes! there were times that I needed to trust, because I didn't have the expertise on hand. But by asking questions and gathering information, I began to feel comfortable with my decisions. I learned along the way.

Build your confidence level and the decisions will take care of themselves. Like I stated before, you may make some decisions that you have the littlest clue on, but still a decision has to be made.

Basic tools, different notes. Preparation and a little trust will carry you a long way.
Example; A vehicle doesn't do what its required to do based on just fuel. It needs different components and definitely maintenance.

Include a little tender loving care.

And you will have a lean mean running machine.

"ENJOY THE RIDE"

Visualize your brain, your body and your soul all as if it were one. Analyze and develop a foundation not outside your brain. Discipline yourself to travel your journey in a prepared and conservative manner.

"BE CAREFUL"

Since we only have 24 hours....

Where will you take yours?

PASSION: Any powerful or compelling emotion or feeling, as love or hate.

The mind is the great equalizer.

Your passion will determine how great the different effects will have on each other. We may have different effects on one another. We still need each other. We are all heading somewhere. **And, we are stronger in numbers. And our numbers will grow.**

Live your own life. Because all the other ones are taken.

14 TRAITS: JJ DID TIE BUCKLE, is the acronym use.
- Justices
- Judgement
- Dependable
- Initiative
- Decisiveness
- Tact
- Integrity
- Endurance
- Bearing
- Unselfishness
- Courage

- Knowledge
- Loyalty
- Enthusiasm

11 PRINCIPLES

1. Know yourself and seek self-improvement.

2. Be technically and tactically proficient.

If and when you can conceal this trait. You may learn the true intentions of others.

3. Develop a sense of responsibility amongst your peers.

4. Make sound and timely decisions.

Do what you are committed too.

5. Set the example. Making sound decisions and owning them will appear in people's perspectives of you. Walk the Talk

6. Know your audience and look out for their welfare. By knowing who you represent your loyalty and commitment will gravitate toward that end.

7. Keep your audience informed. Any time I was in charge of a project. It was very important to keep everyone within the team informed. You are only as strong as the weakest link.

8. Seek responsibility and take responsibility for your action. The more you place your hands on, the more experience you will assemble.

9. Ensure assigned tasks are understood, supervised, and accomplished. By explaining yourself. Clear and concise, will avoid misunderstanding most of the time.

10. Train as a team. Everyone around you is part of your team. Without them you will not be able to advance.

11. Employ your team in accordance with its capabilities. Since everyone is needed for your success, everyone has something to offer. Utilize those skills. Take the meat and leave the bone.

These **Traits** and **Principles are Golden!** Reading each and every one of them, they all play a part in my Goodwill.

"From Family to those who became family."

Give yourself a chance.

Maybe you will get LUCKY.

I'll describe Lucky as; where opportunity and preparation meet.

LUCKY

OPPORTUNITY-----------------PREPAREDNESS

Prepare yourself. You have the tools. Let's put them to profitable use. Let's take a ride and seek out opportunity.

Use these notes wisely.

Always know more than enough. Knowing less than, could lead to places you weren't prepared to enter, so Backup and regroup. I navigated, into many circles. In many different environments. Through right turns and some left turns, my serene travels found many distinguished visits. Amuse yourself. Get involved. Allow the pleasure of your entertainment to occur.

  24 hours is 24 hours

Dad would always say
"Aprende Cómo vivir la Vida"

Learn how to live life.
Simple stuff, Figure it out.

CHAPTER SEVEN

TIME

Time is one of the commodities you will not have control over. We do have a choice on how we invest time. But time can't be used. Time is not tangible. It has no regrets. It expects nothing and it will give you nothing. And once it passes, it will never return. We can lay dormant or began to grow. The actions you take during your time will return some substances, or awareness as a bonus.

Time is a precious commodity. Time management is very important. Invest your time discreetly. Prepare yourself for when the time is right. As you wait for the right moment, assure the time waiting is cultivated while multitasking. As you might find. The direction you wish to move toward may not be ready for you. For whatever reason the people whom you believe are necessary to speak too, are just not willing or available to meet. By doing some homework, or research, reassess your position. As you enjoy your current level or location. you may find a third party who may be willing to help. Someone who may be connected in some form to the person who you are seeking to contact. Sacrifice some time and get involved with them. You might have common interest and acquire a new friend. It might turn out this individual might be the person all along who will get you to your next level of your plan. Let's remember the road map. If one avenue doesn't get you to your desired place, then seek another.

DISCIPLINE: The definition of discipline is defined as 'orderly or prescribed conduct or pattern of behavior'.

Look around and see if it's starting to make sense? I am pretty sure everybody is living their own life. Traveling their own roads. They too, need to cross your path to fulfill their own destination. As you understand yours, you began to understand theirs. During your day of excursions, don't take stuff personally. It's all part of the show.

Let's take a POKER game or any sport as a matter of fact. Take any field you wish to consider and take a moment to think about this. Imagine on how behaviors are displayed. It appears that minimal efforts are shown. Those action have been tried and practiced time and time again. It looks natural, so genuine. That's how good you need to become. Take your show on the road. Cultivate your harvest. And allow your fruit to be the prize.

**SACRIFICE**: AN ACT OF GIVING UP SOMETHING VALUED FOR THE SAKE OF SOMETHING ELSE REGARDED AS MORE IMPORTANT OR WORTHY.

To give up something for something more valuable is a very important concept to obtain. Some of these notes you might already display.

Others, you will gather and treat as your own. These notes have been proven and tested. As I navigated through my excursions. Where I found many doors that have opened and I have entered to view the sight. I lived my own life. Seeking balance. By taking on responsibilities for self-improvement. Sometimes, changes can't be made and other times, changes should be made. But then, you have to factor in people. Not all people understand the concepts of logic. But only know what feels good and makes decisions accordingly. Logical describes something that comes from clear reasoning. The adjective **logical** is rooted in the Greek word logos, which means reason, idea, or words. So, calling something logical means it is based on reason and sound ideas- in other words, thought out with mathematical precision and removed from emotion. Like in the example of the poker player. With some effort and some practice. You will reach the level where your approach of reasoning will become natural, so smooth, and adjust when necessary. Without effort. It might come with some disappointments, but you will need to try and try again. As you grow and become aware of the etiquette of any given situation you may find yourself in. And with some rules and facts (homework). You will understand where the level of reason begins. You can only apply what you know. And if at first you don't succeed, back up figure it out and try again.

Sacrifice will require us to be responsible for our actions. It is incumbent for us to take our responsibility seriously and understand what our responsibility expects of us. In everything you choose to do, you will sacrifice something in return. All of us seek something. What that might be, will depend on the opportunities that have been secured.

Have faith, you'll get there.

This reminds me of a story, where I volunteered to mentor high school students. I'd ask the class this question? By the show of hands, is a drunk on the streets successful? The classroom stood quiet. The expressions on their faces appeared lost. I added, I mean after all he is a drunk, Right!

Not a single hand was raised. So, I responded, with a yes! That the drunk is successful. And they looked at me in an odd fashion. To my imagination, asking me How?

Funny isn't it?
Well, the moral of the story is, if you spent the majority of your time-consuming alcohol, with no reflection and only worry about your next drink, you have chosen to sacrifice normality. You will accomplish what you planned. A plan doesn't need to be written. It only needs to be followed. Worked and cultivated.

And the drunk did just that.

Remember when I stated, don't overstay your welcome, you might just get hooked? Both mentally or physically or spiritually. Stay aware. Enjoy life do what you wish. It's your choice. I am just saying, to analyze yourself and your situation frequently. Live your life. Don't stay idle. Time is probably the only mechanism we have, that we can determine how it will be occupied. Know what skills you pack. Your expertise. Your passion. Do it well and go out and find someone who will reward you for it. Whatever that might be.

By using other options such as, allowing others to complete those tasks you don't enjoy doing, or because of lack of your time. And by Setting priorities. It will expand your free time to be used where it will be more profitable. Use your time wisely.

Someone's garbage, is someone else's treasures.

Learn to be creative. Mix it up. You will find these basic concepts do work in many situations. Stay within the scope of the content.

Keep at point at hand. Stay on task. On your mission.

You have traits, values and principles. You have basic skills. Such as traditional education, Vocation training or specific targeted interest. Use them.

Your goal is only a decision away.

Everybody has 24 hours what you do with it is completely up to you. Ask yourself? How long will you stay? Is this where you would like to be?

- *You have earned it, figure it out.*

CHAPTER EIGHT

FOCUS

: an act of concentrating interest or activity on something.

When you are focused on a given activity, for sure there will be struggles with frustrations and anticipations. If you fall off track along the way, you can always look around and see who the reliable ones are around you. Let them help get you back on track. Remind yourself what you are striving for, and continue in developing your "playground." Know your strengths and plan accordingly. Your strength will derive on your investments or even your losses.

EFFORT *is defined as the exertion of physical or mental power:*

Whichever field you decide to venture on, it will take effort. It will also take your precious time.

You'll find this information will drive you towards your next choice. in whichever direction you plan to go, the amount of effort you put forth will determine how fast you meet your goals. The compensation of your effort will depend on you. It is yours and yours alone.

While reading "Playground of Your Mind" allow your mind to soak in the beauty of this information.
Let's explore the existence within you. It may shed a light on what you already know.

You don't know what you know, until you know what you know. (hindsight is the best foresight.)

PATIENCE: quiet, steady, perseverance, even-tempered care. Diligence.

Having patience is a virtue. It is a necessity in everything you do. Sometimes we are naive to our levels of expectation. That's when we experience overpower of patience. That's when you let your heart detach from your logical thinking, and nothing gets done.

By mastering patience and staying within your scope of expertise. The information acquired or actions viewed could possibly be beneficial toward your next goal.

CHAPTER NINE

COMMUNICATION

The imparting or interchange of thoughts, opinions, or information by speech, writing, or signs.

The definition is very interesting. Let's consider of what actions take place when we communicate.

Everything we say or do is considered communication. By understanding the definition, we will assure we are sending the correct message. Or the message you would like to have interpret.

Let's also take into consideration different cultures may react distant as you speak. It is imperative to evaluate, adjust and find common ground to comprehend each other.
Or, we might intolerantly misunderstand signs when communicating with others, only because

we don't understand. Most of the time, past experiences, perception, and culture background greatly affect the way people talk and behave. Culture plays an important role in shaping the style of communication you choose to use.

A good rule: Speak clear and concise to avoid any misunderstanding by using basic alternatives. Everyone does this, depending on the circumstance or the situation at hand.

Finally, take extra time and follow up with question to confirm you have been understood.

You would like to have your audience embrace what you need to say. But sometimes it just doesn't happen. Have patience and try to understand. By keeping cultural differences in mind can help with this.

Unless people know whom, you are, be cautious with your actions, your clothes, the words that you may choose to use. They Could possibly not take you seriously and may choose to brush you off.

Now you can start to understand why communication is very important to take the time to understand different points of view. Even though you may have developed the Art of Communication, you will still find people who have an emotional wall. They just don't like you. Either way, no matter how much you try, in this case you will not be able to break through. Don't fret over emotionally unstable people for they themselves may not know the reason of their own brain freeze. Give them the respect required and move on.

Communication requires practice.

Ask questions. Confirm.

Remembering respect goes both ways.

To enhance your skill, take a chance. Treat all your opportunities fair. If they don't understand, don't take it personal. Be ready for the answer, or just don't ask the question.

 You will come to realize how you speak to your friends; you won't speak to your family the same way. You may try, but the colloquial develop is truly formed in a different line. Always be aware of your surroundings. You might never know who is listening. This could be one avenue on how gossip gets started.

Once you have developed this skill, your thought process will now take a different form. You will articulate differently depending on your audience. Your words will begin to be selective and your listening skills will enhance. Take the time in waiting for the opportunity to address an issue where circumstances don't require immediate attention.

With these two components. (speaking and listening), you will develop into an effective speaker.

 Like the saying goes, "Don't be jumping onto a moving train." That says, if you don't know what the conversation is about, then stay out. Two's company but three's a crowd

You will also enhance verbal communication and will see that it can be used to gather information without any direct question. Think about this. Hmm.

If you are not ready for the answer, don't ask the question.

Communication is an art. The discipline of exercising this gift is essential. By getting to understand how we are intertwined in this world. As when asking a question and communicated clearly. Also Because you took the time to understand.

Your journey will continue forward without regrets or sadness because You showed the respect required.   Maybe there will be some disappointments only because the outcome didn't turn out to your expectations. But it wasn't because you didn't try to the best of your ability. Or you did not take the time to understand and use the required etiquette approach, it happens. There are many styles in communicating. Select yours and hope for the best.

Learn it, know it, make it a habit.

Effective communication is twofold. Listening as well as speaking. Many people will try to formulate an answer when they should be listening. Rest assured they will miss the important points of what is being conveyed. This is critical if the speaker has only a short time to express his message and without providing a question, period. A perfect example, when I was Grunting with those hard-core Vietnam Vets. The main goal was, mission accomplishment. Yes, we had our sights set. But then came all that intricate information to getting there. It does no one any good if we don't understand the plan on the set goal, or final outcome. So, listen because time might be of essence. And the information is not up for discussion.

Listen when you should be listening.

During the course of my military career, as one of my fellow partners approached me.
I asked him a simple question. "Hey what's up?" His immediate response was,
"You ask that to ask what?"
I sat there on the bench in a blank stare for a second. With curiosity I looked him straight in his eye and asked, "Why did you ask that?"
His reply, "Well Rafael, Many times people don't ask what they really want to know. So to minimize confusion, and waste of time, let's get to the real question."

Hum, interesting.

Whether you choose to listen or speak, it's your choice. I have been told; we should do more listening than speaking. That's why we have two ears.

CHAPTER TEN

POLITICS

When I was elected and entrusted to oversee the finances of a city as the Mayor, I took on a considerable amount of responsibility. I had to continually do homework to educate myself and stay prepared and on point. I did sacrifice time away from my family to be available to the community as needed on their time.

Always planning for the future while considering the present. We only have so much money in the coffers. Assure all services are organized and maintained. And with the remaining balance, determine where we will grow and how to invest in bettering the community. I took my responsibilities seriously. When I made a decision, I could back it up with concrete data. We had a team and we knew our expectations.

I give credit to my military experience. Due to the fact of the discipline instilled in me. From those Vietnam Veterans and the officers who provided encouragement and opportunities. During this experience I came to realize, I was capable of handling more than I expected. I was also better prepared than I realized. if I had not chosen to take on this adventure I would have never felt the pleasure this experience gave me. In being responsible for the citizens of this community and also assuring their confidence in me was well worth the effort. I took a calculated chance, and it paid off. I am thankful for the opportunity in displaying my skills in every given moment. And used every tool necessary in order to move forward. because I am for the people, of the people.

Being the Mayor meant leading by example and the discipline to perform to the expectations of those around me.
As the Mayor of any community requires integrity and assurance of taking care of the

people's needs first. This type of volunteering doesn't come with tangible rewards. But it is self-fulfilling. The beauty of knowing you have stood true to your word in watching out for the people's needs.

Being sincere and assured that all decisions are in the best interest of the city. And not individuals. By facts alone any decisions can be made, but many things need to be considered. Such as, who created that situation? Why was it created? Or what caused the outcome? What was expected? Where did it end up? When did this take place?
Keep the 5Ws method in mind and always ask the questions. Who, What, Where, When, and Why? Most likely you will arrive at a good decision.

A question never asked, will never be answered. No action is action within itself.

My state of mind was always as such. From trusting people, to my integrity. By dealing with facts and setting priorities I find to be good policy. You cannot fix a problem if you don't know where it lies. By having experience in any given field, you will give yourself a cutting edge over the rest. To understand what is legitimate and the fortitude to ask questions when necessary.

It does take courage to do the right thing. In politics you could possibly find yourself thinking to be more than you really are. Stay humble and make the best choice for the people and everything will work out at the end. We are here to serve them. Every tree can be told by the fruit that it bears. It is very easy to carry a title and do nothing, then expect greatness. When you hold a role to play, do it well, be responsible and be accountable.
For the weak will allow you to face the burden of their decisions.

I did ask and was approved by a fair election to oversee an organization and manage with the required duties. It was also expected of me to give guidance and share my expertise. I questioned anything being considered for the betterment of the whole. As a team member I assured the others were well verse and equally a part of the decision making process. We always consider past actions, present situations, and future plans. Those key ideas were always kept in consideration in every decision.

SIRACH 27; 4-7
6. The fruit discloses the cultivation of a tree; So the expression of a thought discloses the cultivation of a man's mind.(RSVCE)

Here is where your communications skills will be a necessity.

When in doubt, figure it out.
Don't be a flake, investigate.

Many things don't change, only people do. Take advantage of learning. You can learn as you grow, as you travel, don't remain in one place too long for that's all you will come to know. I don't mean physically. Take advantage of every moment that life has to offer. It came across your path for a reason.

Enjoy the moment in time.

CHAPTER ELEVEN

CONSEQUENCES: _a result or effect of an action or condition._

Make calculated decisions. No one is saying you can't play here or there. Use your common sense. Those are based on the knowledge that you have acquired this far and use it to its full potential. You have earned it. Put your knowledge to task.

You may have the freedom of choice, but not the freedom of the consequent.

Living life is free. Choices are yours. The decision-making process is your responsibility. keep it updated.

UNDERSTANDING will be the most difficult part of the decisions you make. As you pursue your choices, you will have trials or hardships you must endure.

Consequences? Well, there are consequences. These can be positive or they can be negative. Depending on your choices, or your techniques. A consequence is a natural reaction to the action one put forth beforehand.

When you think you know it all, you just might be wrong.

It's our responsibility to seek the way.

CHAPTER TWELVE

CLOSURE

"At the end of the day"

Thanks again for everything, your effort and time and expertise. I have enjoyed this ride!

To think at 53 years of age I would be retired. For me, is just not believable. But it took place at the right time. With a plan in place and a good solid direction, and all those folks willing to help, many things are possible. I had my trials and frustrations. But now I understand those were necessary in fulfilling my next mission in life.

I am truly thankful for all the opportunities the Lord has given to me. I put my experiences to task and adjusted accordingly as needed. The plan that was put in place during those times has come to fruition. And I am prepared for my next endeavors to come. But for now I will enjoy my time with family, friends and those I will meet along the way. It is difficult to explain from where I sit now, so I won't. As the saying goes;

If I have to explain you probably wouldn't understand.

As I was building the playground of my mind, My wife Lorraine was building a very nice, warm home. Without her continuous support, it is possible I wouldn't be sharing these helpful notes.

As a retiree I can say it is truly comfortable to be able to call a place, home. Because of her efforts and caring, she helped build a home we both as a team did strive for. And I am thankful for her partnership in this venture. We now spend as much time as possible with our grandchildren and our family as a whole. We enjoy the moments given to us, to help raise our grandchildren. As well as enjoying all the good times we brought along with us, where it includes our friends. At times it was a challenge, but today I can say it is worth the effort to understand and enjoy your life. And help others to enjoy theirs.

1. We help teach and train and prepare our grandchildren.
2. We guide and assure communications are clear and understood. Lorraine, outside of the boy's mother, plays the majority role of guiding them.
3. She is what keeps balance in our home. I always have to remember; she built our home and has more knowledge of what is necessary to continue a loving place to rest. She was truly heaven sent!

Me, I always stay available when assistance is necessary. Or better yet, when I am directed to do! Ha-ha-ha, LOL

Acknowledgements

"I am glad friendship doesn't come with price tags. For if it does, I'd never afford someone as great as you."

Pinterest.

Maslow's Hierarchy of needs.

Abraham Maslow.

Live your own life, Not someone else's.

Entrepreneur.

11 Principles.

The Military Leader>
principles-military

14 traits.

The Military Leader>
Principles-military

Values

Military core values

Logical Person.
Vocabulary.com>dictionary>logical

Culture Barriers.
https;//www.businesstopia.net>culture-b

If I have to explain you wouldn't understand
ASCCC

Sirach 27:4-7
6. RSVCE
Dictionary/Thesaurus on line
Dictionary.com

Special thanks to:
Those who took time out of their busy
schedule to proof read and share ideas.

My Daughter Mona Melendez for her critical
reading and thinking skills.

My Aunt Emma Hillend. Retired. For her craft
in reading.

My Niece Reyna Melendez. ASU graduate
Bachelor of Arts. Interdisciplinary Studies
w/emphasis in Spanish and Mass
Communications. Master in Education.

To Scott Brown. Without him I just might not
have completed this book.
      After a very long period of time, without
communication. Scott dropped me a text and
asked, are you ready to finish the book. Very

Honorable person. The encouragement I needed to kickstart my motivation.

Thank you.

Made in the USA
Coppell, TX
28 January 2022

72546402R00063